O9-BUD-258

Also by Charles Addams

9201   01 589356   01 7   (IC=1)
ADDAMS. CHARLES.   10/13/83
CREATURE COMFORTS
(B) C1981 0741.5973ADDAMS

OCT 2 3 1989

1989

Chas Addams
Creature Comforts

Simon and Schuster • New York

COPYRIGHT © 1981 BY CHARLES ADDAMS
ALL RIGHTS RESERVED
INCLUDING THE RIGHT OF REPRODUCTION
IN WHOLE OR IN PART IN ANY FORM
PUBLISHED BY SIMON AND SCHUSTER
A DIVISION OF GULF & WESTERN CORPORATION
SIMON & SCHUSTER BUILDING
ROCKEFELLER CENTER
1230 AVENUE OF THE AMERICAS
NEW YORK, NEW YORK 10020
SIMON AND SCHUSTER AND COLOPHON ARE TRADEMARKS OF
SIMON & SCHUSTER

MANUFACTURED IN THE UNITED STATES OF AMERICA

1   3   5   7   9   10   8   6   4   2

LIBRARY OF CONGRESS CATALOGING IN PUBLICATION DATA

ADDAMS, CHARLES.
CREATURE COMFORTS.
1.   AMERICAN WIT AND HUMOR, PICTORIAL.
I.   TITLE
NC1429.A25A4   1981   741.5'973   81-8921
                                            AACR2
ISBN 0-671-43835-2

All the drawings in this book, including those on the endpapers
and the jacket, appeared originally in *The New Yorker* and were
copyrighted © 1976, 1977, 1978, 1979, 1980, 1981 by The New
Yorker Magazine, Inc.

FOR TEE TIGGER ALICE
MACY AND NEW DOG

"*I think you know everybody.*"

"Inflationary pressures oblige us to reduce expenditures. Therefore, the following three staff members shall be dismissed."

"Do you know 'Hickory Dickory Dock'?"

"He's in the garden."

"*Actually, Mitchell was a pioneer in the whole white-wine thing.*"

"So we've discovered the Fountain of Youth. Who's going to sail the old tub back?"

"The usual."

"*Now that we've given up the car, I wonder if we still need Orkins.*"

"*I just got tired of the same old hat.*"

"*You're seeing another woman, aren't you, Robert?*"

"*I keep getting this feeling we're being watched.*"

"*For some reason, I suddenly have this cult following.*"

"It's a town that time forgot."

"*I'm taking you off blackbird pie, Sire.*"

"It's going to be great! All natural ingredients."

"*Not bad for an old man. How are you?*"

"*I don't think I love farming the way you do, Dad.*"

"All right, Carruthers, what's on our agenda for today?"

"*This all your own stuff, fella?*"

"Why can't we go to the mountains this year?"

"Notice how the eyes seem to keep following you?"

"'The Scourge of Civilization'! Me? Are you kidding?"

"This had better be good, Robinson!"

"*And this is Stephen's den.*"

"*Thompson, find out how many people I had to
step on to get to the top.*"

"Hi! I'm Big Brother, and I'm running for President in '84."

"*There's no cause for panic, Mrs. Munson, but, frankly, there
are certain indicators that cannot be ignored.*"

"I'm sorry, Travers, but I'm going to have to let you go."

"How can you just lie there and <u>accept</u> continental drift?"

"Mrs. Wilcox? I think you'll be happy to hear
we've recovered your stolen car."

"To . . . hell . . . with . . . yogurt."

"We're looking for people who like to write."

"Don't worry. They'll be out by the tenth."

Separated at birth, the Mallifert twins meet accidentally.

"We're both pretty rotten, but I'm generally considered
the lesser of the two evils."

"From the island of J. P. Widmer III."

"Oh, nothing much, Frank. What's new with you?"

"Now, should you decide to join our organization you will be surrendering certain liberties."

"*This is Rodney's room.*"

"One gets used to the flying fishes, but that bloody dawn
coming up like thunder is driving me crackers."

"First a drink, Margaret. Then we'll talk."

"High-test."

"'Il Penseroso,' by John Milton."

"What the hell's come over Monahan?"

"*How long has the light been out in the fridge, Mabel?*"

"*Finally, Howard said I had to choose between him and ceramics.*"